Knots

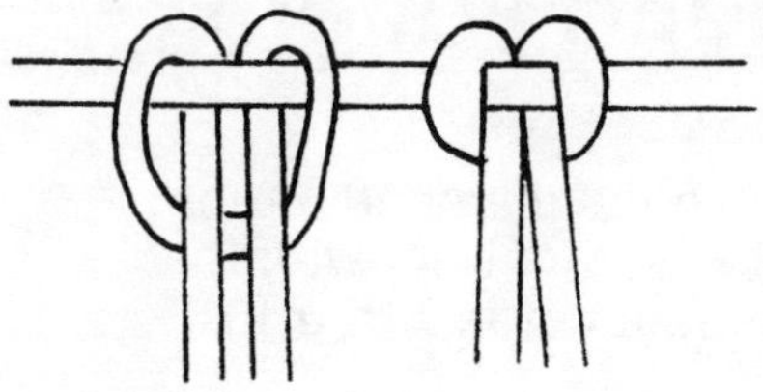

Reverse Lark's Head

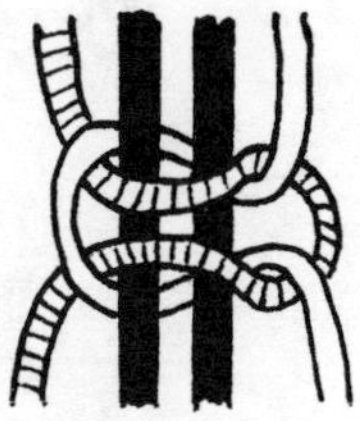

Left Square Knot

Right Square Knot

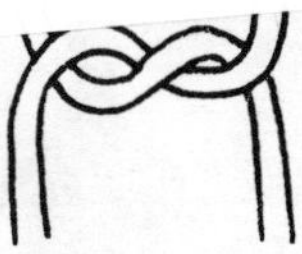

Half Knot

Square Knot Sinnet

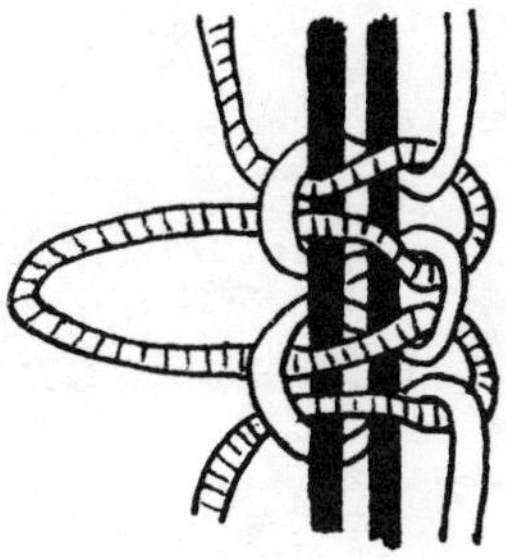

Left Hand Picot

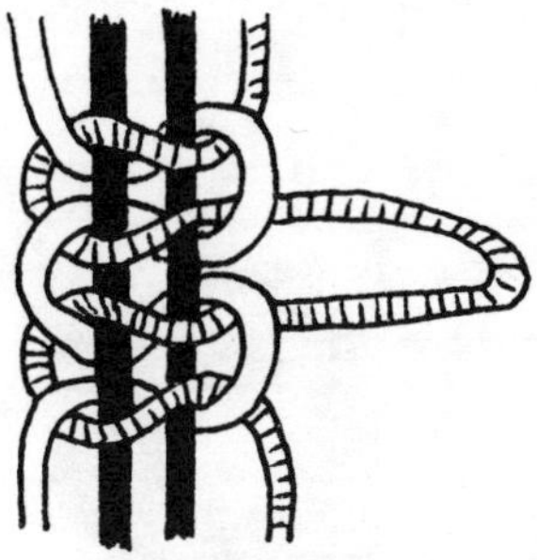

Right Hand Picot

Half Knot Sinnet

Overhand Knot

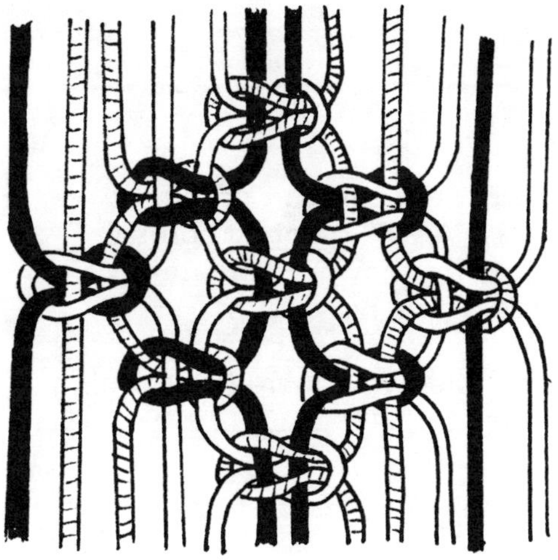

Alternating Square Knot

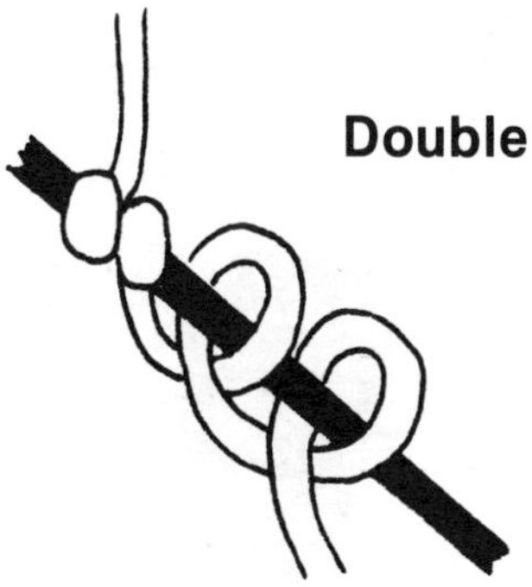

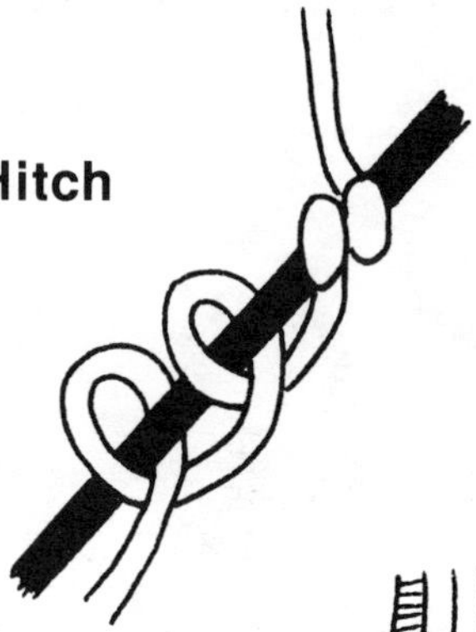

Double Half Hitch

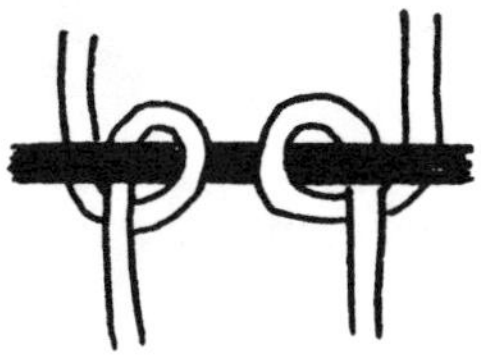

Half Hitch

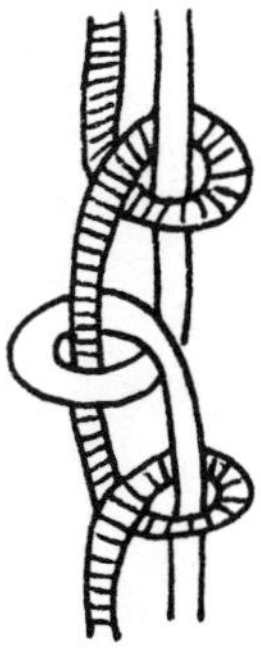

Alternating Half Hitch

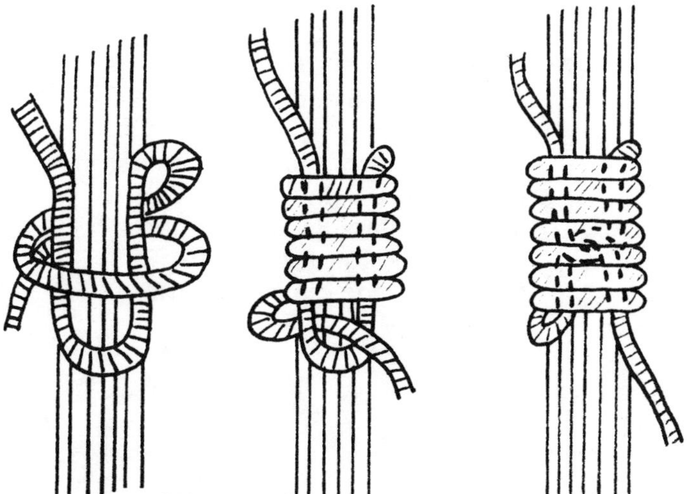

Wrap

To make macrame easy, slip a gingham covered macrame board under a clip board.

1

2

Diamond Pattern

1 To begin the diamond pattern: make a Square Knot with the center four cords 7 thru 10.

2 Row 2: tie a Square Knot using cords 5 thru 8. Tie another Square Knot using cords 9 thru 12.

3

4

3 Row 3: tie a Square Knot using cords 3 thru 6. Tie another Square Knot with cords 11 thru 14.

4 Row 4: tie a Square Knot with cords 1 thru 4 and another Square Knot with cords 13 thru 16.

5

6

5 Row 5: tie a Square Knot using cords 4 AND 13 around cords 5 thru 12 as shown. Straighten cords 5 thru 12.

6 Row 6: tie two Square Knots using cords 1 thru 4 and 13 thru 16.

7

8

7 Row 7: tie two Square Knots with cords 3 thru 6 and 11 thru 14.

8 Row 8: tie two Square Knots using cords 5 thru 8 and 9 thru 12. Row 9: tie a Square Knot using the center four cords 7 thru 10. This completes the diamond pattern.

Single Towel Holder

YOU WILL NEED:

one 3″ plastic ring
one 5″ plastic ring
16 yards 5-6mm cord
one ceramic butterfly (this one is 2″ long)

1

2

1 Cut the cord into eight pieces each 2 yards long. Fold each cord in half and attach to the 3″ plastic ring using a Reverse Lark's Head.

2 Follow steps 1 thru 4 on page 2 to make half the diamond pattern.

3

4

3 With cords 4 AND 13 tie half a Square Knot around cords 5 thru 12.

4 Slip the ceramic butterfly onto cords 7 thru 10. Complete the Square Knot underneath the butterfly.

5

6

5 Complete the diamond pattern by following steps 6 thru 8 on page 2.

6 Double Half Hitch the center four cords onto the 5″ plastic ring.

7

8

7 Flip the ring up as shown. Repeat the diamond pattern on page 2.

8 To finish the bottom: lay the first cord at a diagonal as shown. Double Half Hitch cords 2, 3, 4, 5, 6, 7, and 8 onto the first cord.

9

10

9 Lay the last cord at a diagonal as shown. Double Half Hitch cords 15, 14, 13, 12, 11, 10, 9 and 1 onto the last cord.

10 Repeat steps 8 and 9.

11

12

11 Trim the ends to desired length, these are 6″ long.

12 Tie an Overhand Knot in the end of each cord.

Toilet Paper Holder

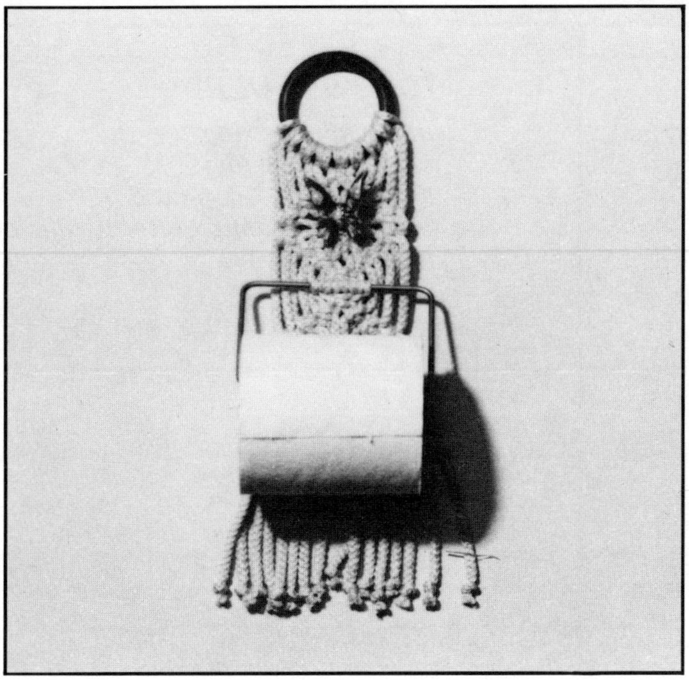

YOU WILL NEED:

16 yards 5-6mm cord
one 3″ plastic ring
ceramic butterfly (this one is 2″ long)
one 5″ × 7″ wire rectangle OR wire paper holder from a hardware store
wire cutters
pliers
paint for use on metal

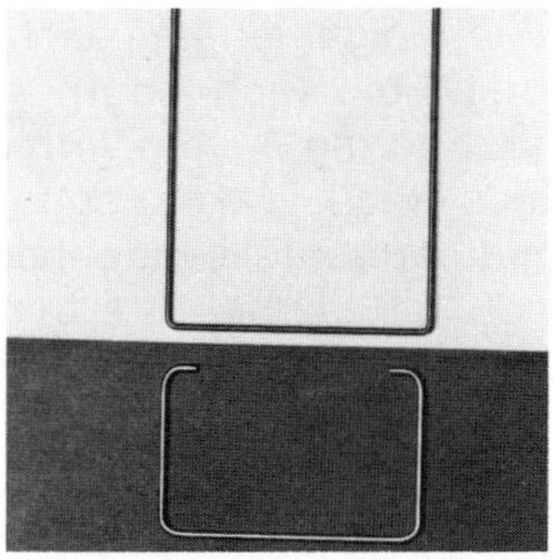

1

2

1 To make the toilet paper wire: cut the 5″ × 7″ wire rectangle in half. Use the pliers to bend each end in ½″. Paint any desired color using three coats of paint.

2 Cut the cord into eight pieces each 2 yards long. Fold each cord in half and attach to the plastic ring with a Reverse Lark's Head. Repeat steps 2 thru 5 on pages 3 and 4.

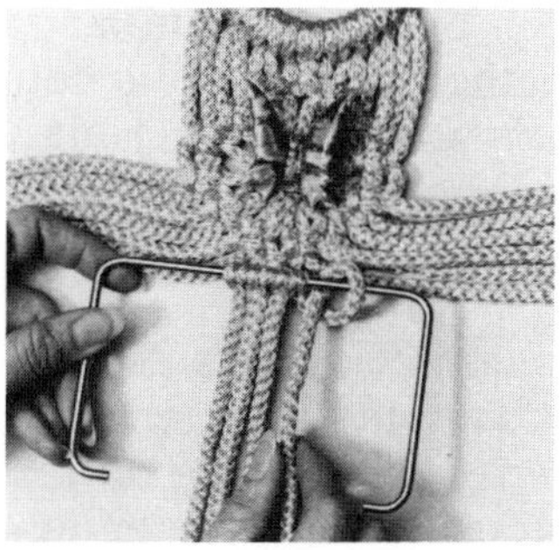

3

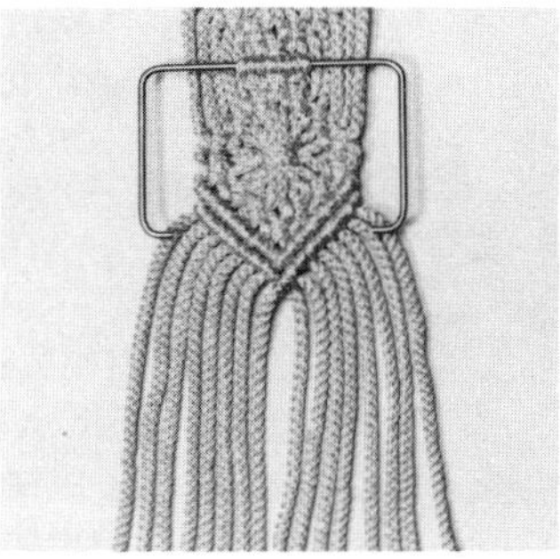

4

3 To attach the toilet paper wire: lay the wire as shown and attach the center 4 cords with a Double Half Hitch. Be sure the wire is centered on the macrame.

4 To complete the toilet paper repeat steps 7 thru 12 on page 4.

Double Towel Holder

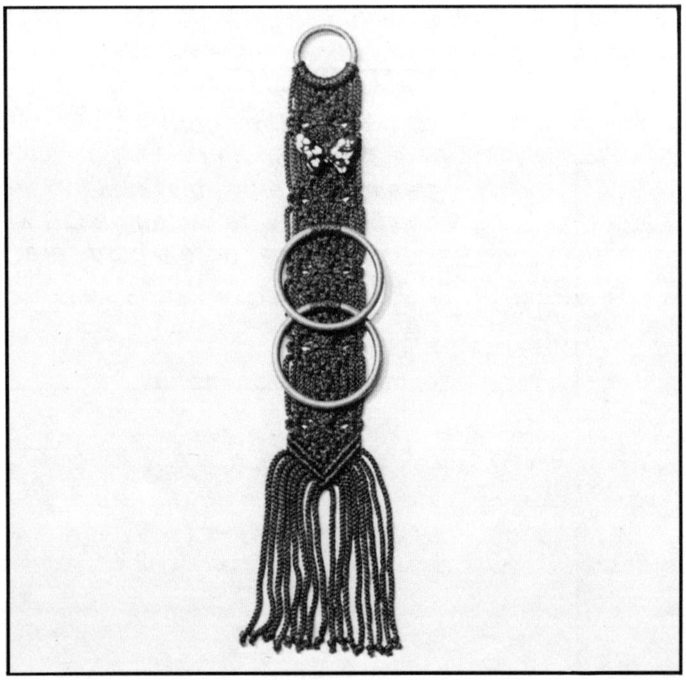

YOU WILL NEED:

one 3″ plastic ring
two 5″ plastic rings
26 yards of 5-6mm cord
one large ceramic butterfly (this one is 3″ across)

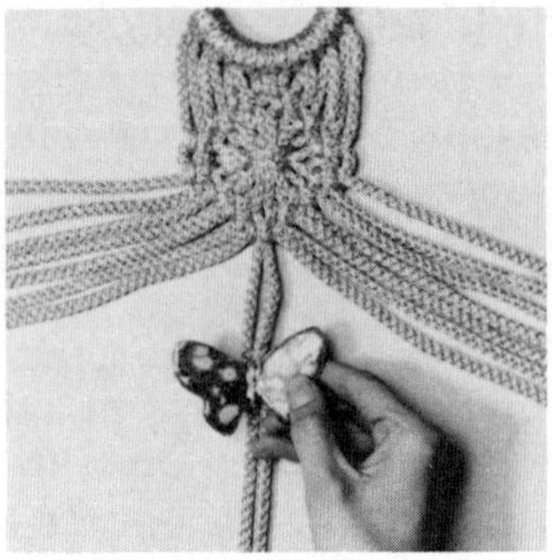

1

2

1 Cut the cord into eight lengths each 3¼ yards long. Fold each length in half and attach to the 3″ ring with a Reverse Lark's Head. Make a complete diamond pattern following the steps on page 2. Slip the butterfly onto cords 8 and 9.

2 Make another complete diamond pattern. Attach one 5″ ring to the center four cords with a Double Half Hitch.

3

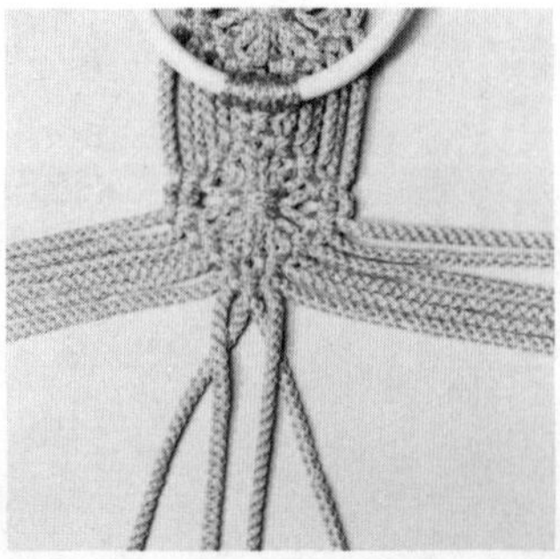

4

3 Make another diamond pattern. Attach the other 5″ ring to the center four cords with a Double Half Hitch. Make one more diamond pattern.

4 Reverse the center 4 cords as shown. Make another diamond pattern. Then, complete the project following steps 8 thru 12 on page 4.

Towel Rack

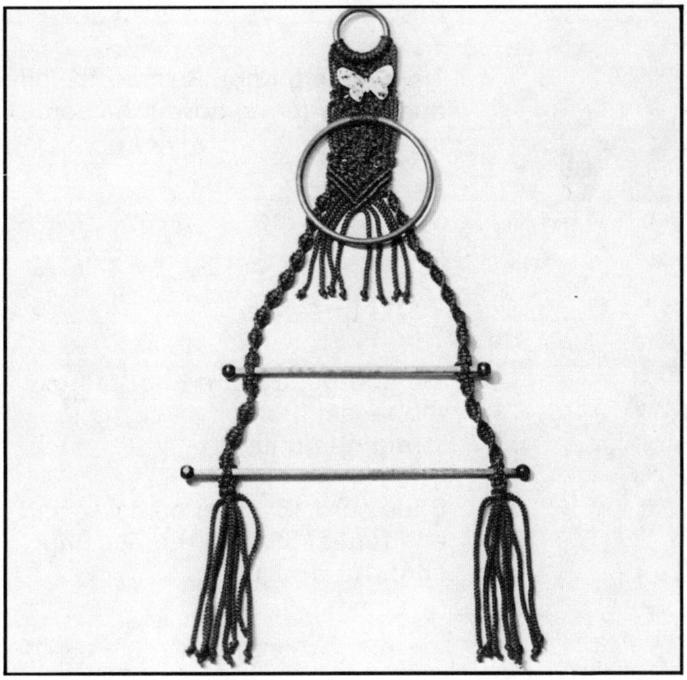

YOU WILL NEED:

one 3″ plastic ring
one 7″ plastic ring
one large ceramic butterfly (this one is 3″ across)
25 yards of 5-6mm cord
one 3/8″ wide dowel 13″ long
one 3/8″ wide dowel 17″ long
four ¾″ wide (20mm) wooden beads
t-pins
craft glue
optional: paint for the dowels

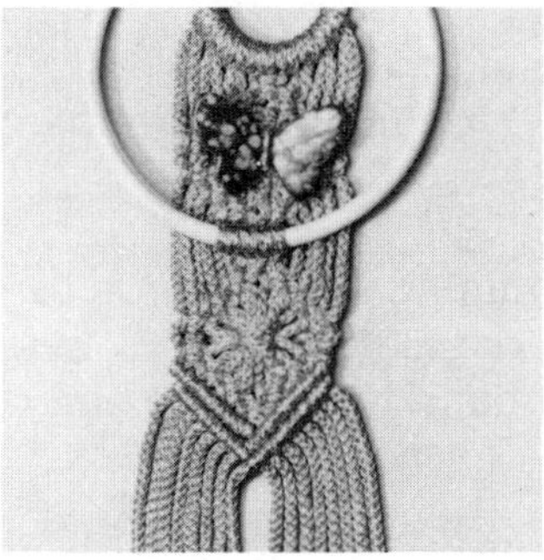

1

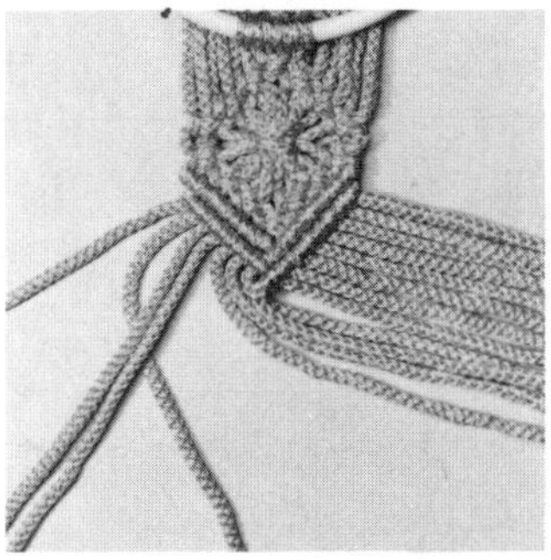

2

1 Cut the cord as follows: four cords each 18″ long (save these to make the tassels), four each 1⅔ yards long, two each 2½ yards long and two cords each 5½ yards long. Fold the cords in half and attach to the 3″ plastic ring in the following order—1⅔ yard, 5½ yard, 2½ yard, 1⅔ yard, 1⅔ yard, 2½ yard and 1⅔ yard. Follow steps 2 thru 10 on pages 3 and 4 (for the Single Towel Holder).

2 Slide the second cord under cords 3 and 4 as shown.

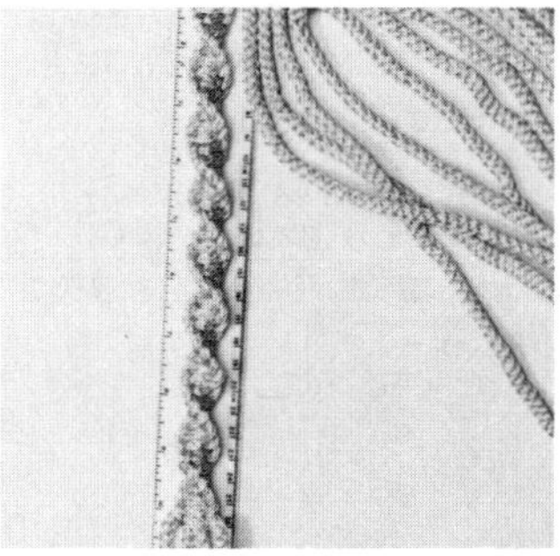

3

4

3 Tie a 10″ long Half Knot Sinnet using cords 1, 2, 3, and 4. Make a Square Knot.

4 Leave a ½″ space and tie a Square Knot. Make a 4″ long Half Knot Sinnet. Tie another Square Knot. Leave a ½″ space, then make another Square Knot.

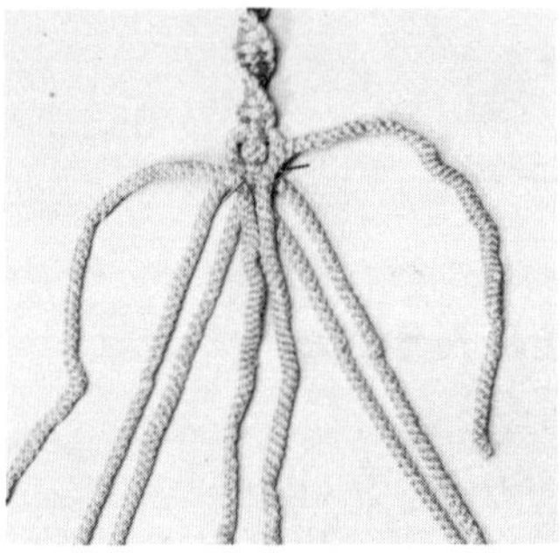

5

6

5 To make a tassel: fold two of the 18″ cords in half. Pin the center of each cord directly under the last Square Knot.

6 Tie a Square Knot. Remove the pins and lower (bring down) the cords as shown.

7

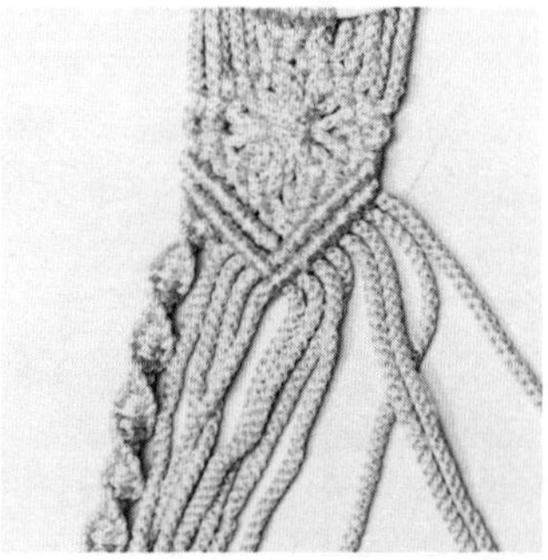

8

7 Tie another Square Knot to hold the tassel. Pull on all cords to straighten them.

8 Slide cord 15 under cords 13 and 14 and repeat steps 3 thru 7 using cords 13 thru 16.

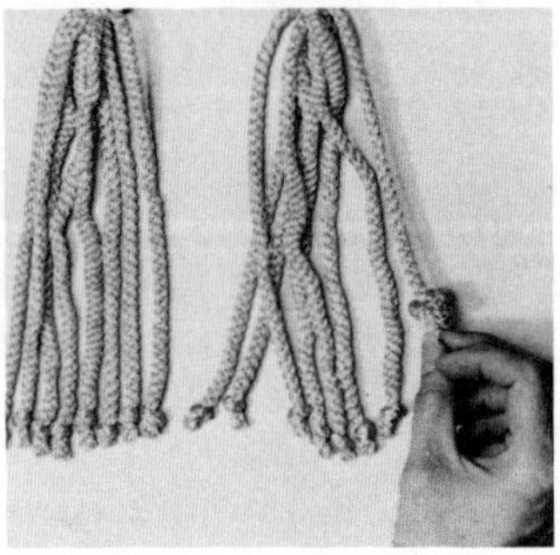

9

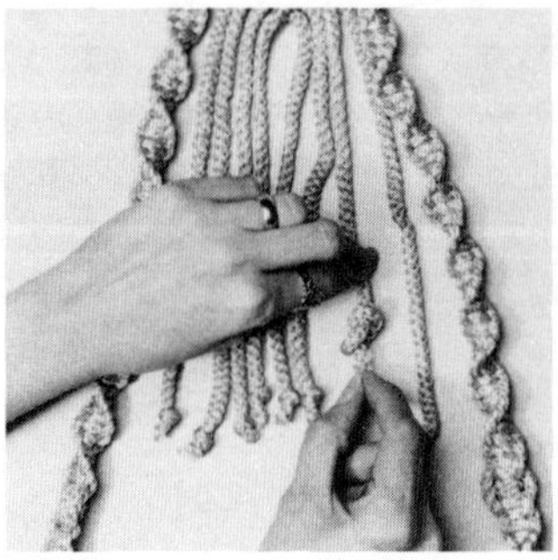

10

9 Cut the tassels to desired length (these are 8″ long). Tie an Overhand Knot at the end of each cord.

10 Cut the remaining center cords to the desired length, these are 6″ long. Use an Overhand Knot at the end of each cord.

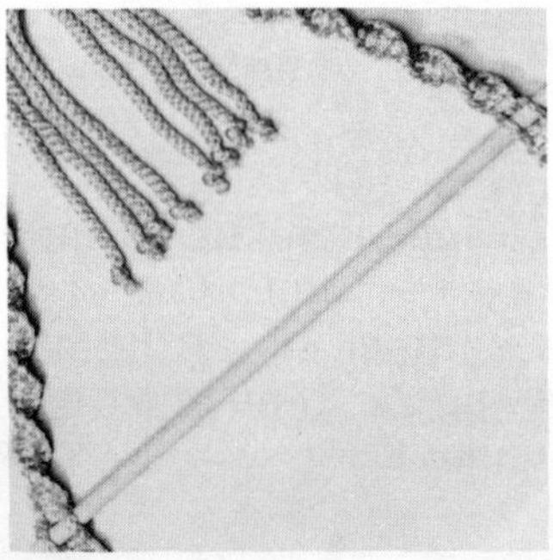

11

12

11 Slip the 12″ dowel into the first ½″ space on each side.

12 Slip the 18″ dowel into the second ½″ space on each side. Glue on a wooden bead to each end of the dowels.

Tooth Brush Holder

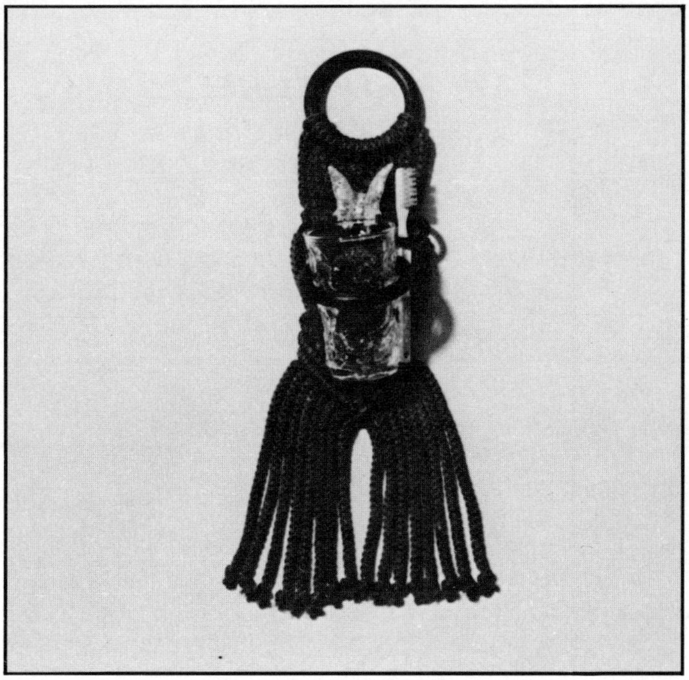

YOU WILL NEED:

two 3″ plastic rings
two 1″ to 1¼″ wide plastic rings (check at needle craft or drapery stores)
one ceramic butterfly (this one is 2″ across)
16 yards of 5-6mm cord

1

2

3

4

1 Cut eight pieces of cord each 2 yards long. Fold each cord in half and attach to one of the 3″ plastic rings with a Reverse Lark's Head. Make half the diamond pattern following steps 1 thru 4 on page 2. With cords 4 AND 13 tie half a Square Knot around cords 5 thru 12. Slide the butterfly onto cords 7 thru 10. Complete the Square Knot under the butterfly.

2 Slide one 1¼″ plastic ring onto cords 2 and 3. Loop the cords as shown using a Single Half Hitch.

3 Attach the other 1¼″ plastic ring onto cords 14 and 15. Tie a Square Knot under each ring and pull cords 2, 3, 14 and 15 to tighten the ring.

4 Complete the diamond pattern following steps 7 and 8 on page 2. Attach the other 3″ plastic ring onto the center four cords using a Double Half Hitch. Make another diamond pattern and finish the piece following steps 7 thru 12 on page 4.

Macrame Accent

YOU WILL NEED:

one 3″ plastic ring
one large ceramic butterfly (3″ across)
dried flowers for filler
5 small silk flowers with 2 leaves
1 yard ribbon 1½″ wide (#9)
16 yards 5-6mm cord
craft glue

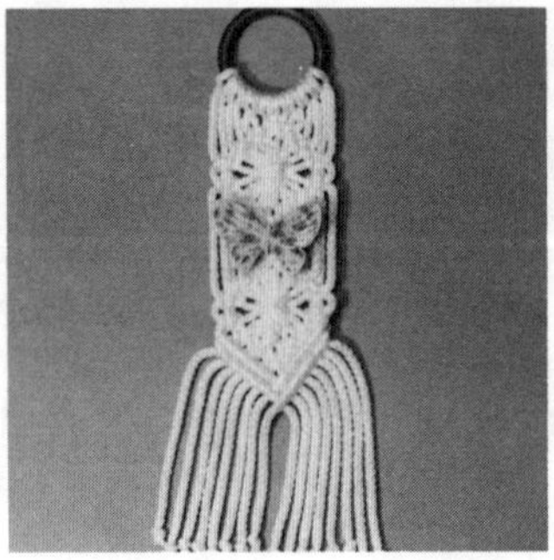

1

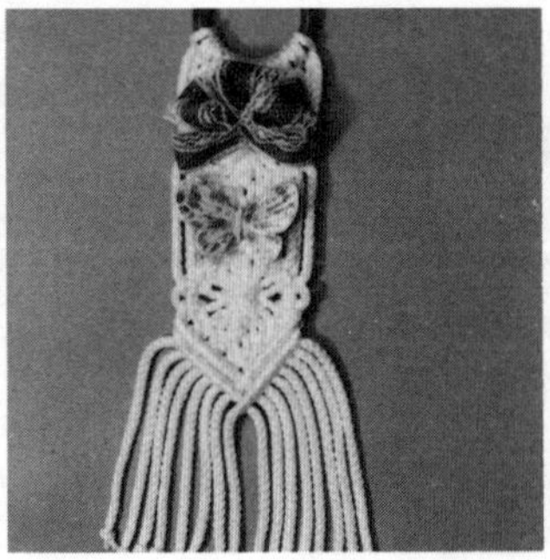

2

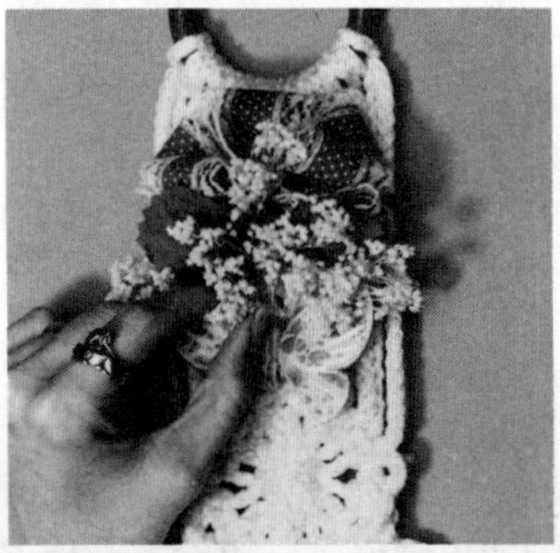

3

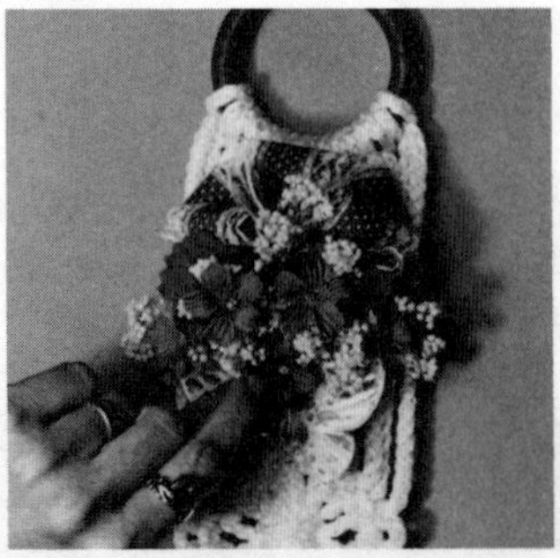

4

1 Cut the cord into eight pieces each 2 yards long. Fold each cord in half and attach to the plastic ring using a Reverse Lark's Head. Make a diamond pattern following the directions on page 2. Slip the ceramic butterfly onto the 2 center cords. Make another diamond pattern. Finish following steps 8 thru 12 on page 4.

2 Make a 4″ wide bow (see inside back cover). Cut off the excess wire. Glue the bow just above the center of the diamond.

3 Cut off 2 leaves, dip the ends in glue and place just below the bow. Cut sprigs of filler flower to 3″ long. Dip the cut end in glue and insert between the bow and butterfly. Cut more filler 2″ long, dip in glue and position on top of the longer filler.

4 Cut the silk flowers so they are 2″ long, dip in glue and add to the filler.

Wall Planter

YOU WILL NEED:

one 3″ plastic ring
one ceramic butterfly (this one is 2″ long)
one 4″ tall fish bowl
20 yards of 5–6mm cord
ruler

1

2

1 Cut the cord into eight lengths each 2½ yards long. Fold each cord in half and attach to the plastic ring using a Reverse Lark's Head. Follow steps 2 thru 4 on page 3 and step 5 on page 4. Reverse the center 4 cords.

2 Make a second diamond pattern as shown on page 2.

3

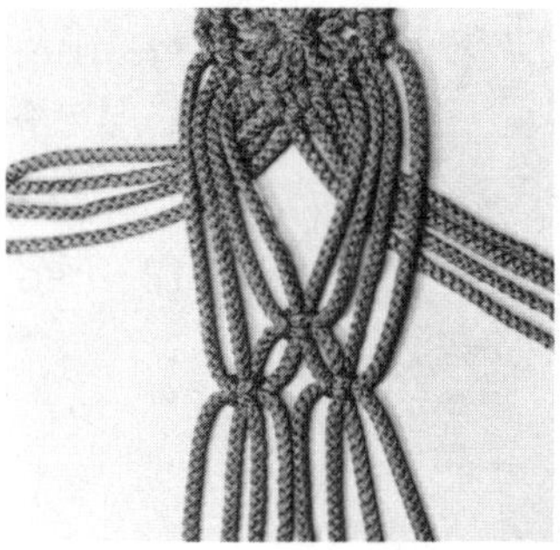

4

3 Drop down 4″ and tie a Square Knot with cords 3, 4, 13 and 14.

4 Drop down an additional 1″ and tie a Square Knot with cords 1 thru 4 and 13 thru 16. Lay this section aside.

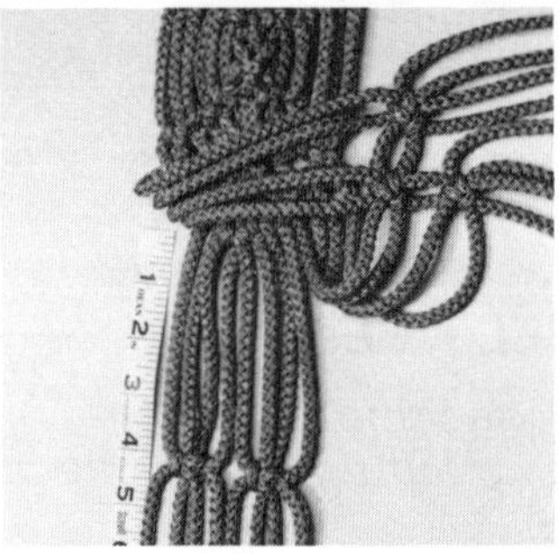

5

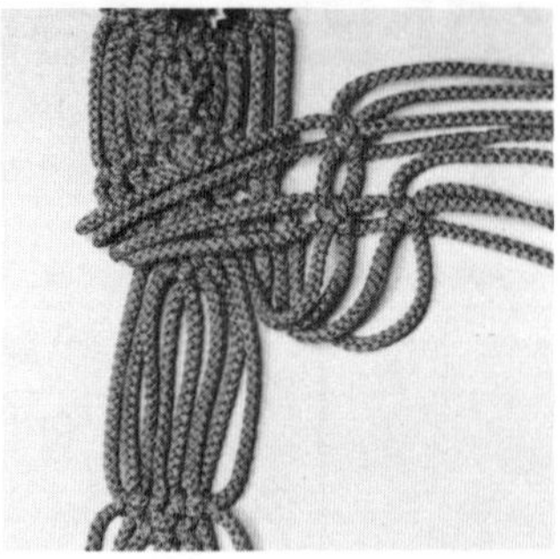

6

5 Drop down 4″ and tie two Square Knots using cords 5 thru 8 and 9 thru 12.

6 Tie a Square Knot with the center four cords 7 thru 10.

7

8

7 Place the two sections together and tie a Square Knot with 2, 1, 5, and 6 as shown.

8 Tie another Square Knot using cords 11, 12, 16 and 15.

9

10

9 Finish by tying a Square Knot with the center four cords, forming a circle.

10 Alternate and tie 4 more Square Knots around the circle.

11

12

11 Trim the cords to the desired length, these are 9″ long. Tie an Overhead Knot at the end of each cord.

12 Insert the fish bowl.

The Seagull Windchime with ceramic and brass bells.

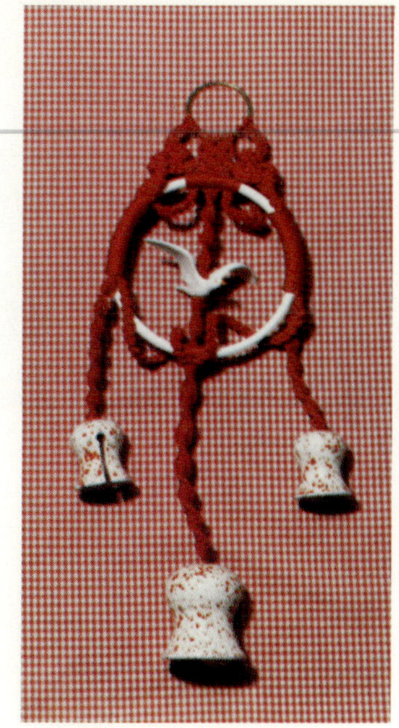

On the left a Seasonal Swag using brass bells without the Alternating Half Hitch Sinnets. The Swag on the right is made with 9mm cord.

When making the Toothbrush Holder a spring clip can be added to hold a tube of toothpaste or use three small rings for toothbrushes instead of a ring for a glass.

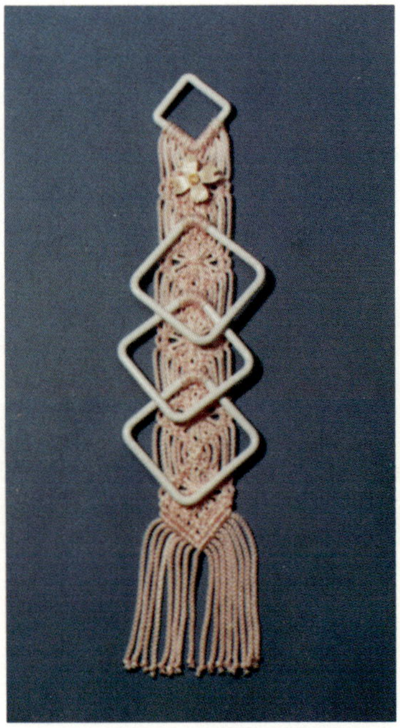

A Triple Towel Holder.

A bathroom set using silk flowers and lace instead of a ceramic butterfly.

The Wall Planter can hold guest soaps as well as plants or even a gold fish.

Three Door Chimes—
one with a brushed tail.

A Christmas
collection.

Three drapery
hooks to hold keys.

An aqua Wall
Planter with silk
flowers, it could
also hold a fresh
flower bouquet.

Ready for baby!

A clothespin makes this piece a recipe holder.

This kitchen ensemble is made with 5mm cord.

Macrame Accents in many colors.

The Double Towel Holder is also useful in the kitchen.

Note Pad Holder

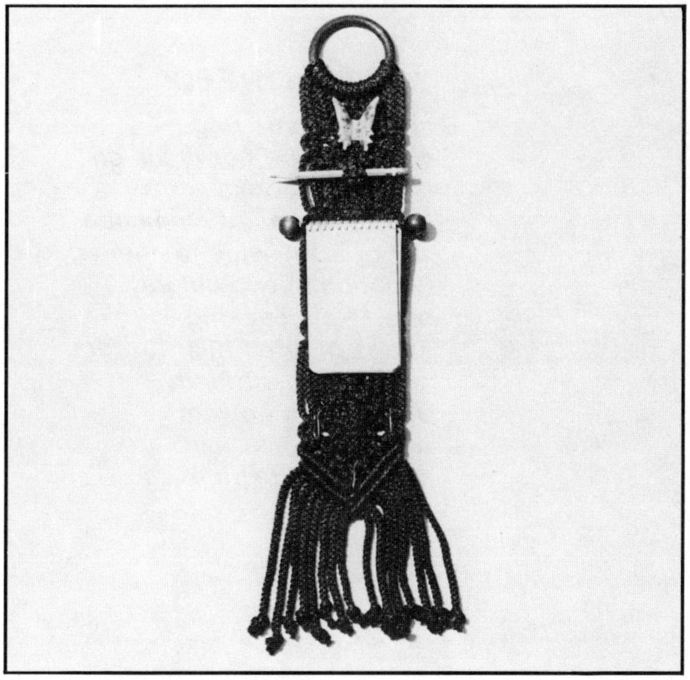

YOU WILL NEED:

one 3" plastic ring
one ceramic butterfly (this one is 2" long)
pencil
one 3" × 5" spiral note pad
4½" length of ¼" dowel
24 yards of 5–6mm cord
3 pin-on drapery hooks

1

2

1 Cut eight cords each 3 yards long. Fold each cord in half and attach to the plastic ring with a Reverse Lark's Head. Follow steps 2 thru 4 on page 3 and step 5 on page 4. With the center four cords tie four Square Knots.

2 Take the middle 2 cords and insert just above the Square Knots. Pull to form a loop thus making a Square Knot Button.

3

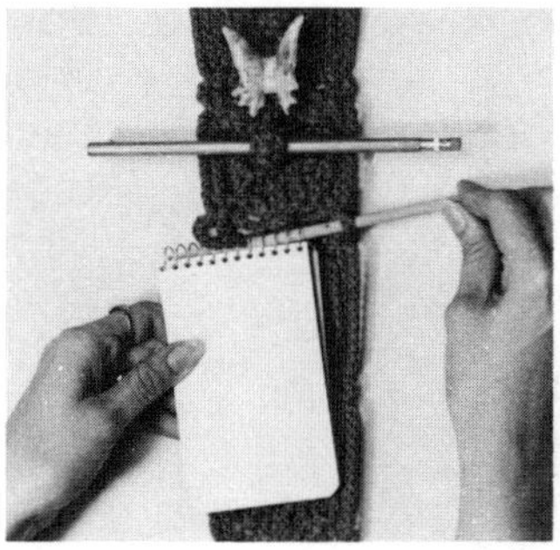

4

3 Tie a Square Knot to secure the Square Knot Button. Pull the center two cords to tighten the loop.

4 Make three diamond patterns. Be sure to reverse the center 4 cords between each diamond pattern, see page 6, step 4. Finish following steps 8 thru 12 on page 4. Insert the pencil and use the dowel to hold the note pad in place. The drapery hooks are used to hold notes or keys.

Cup Holder

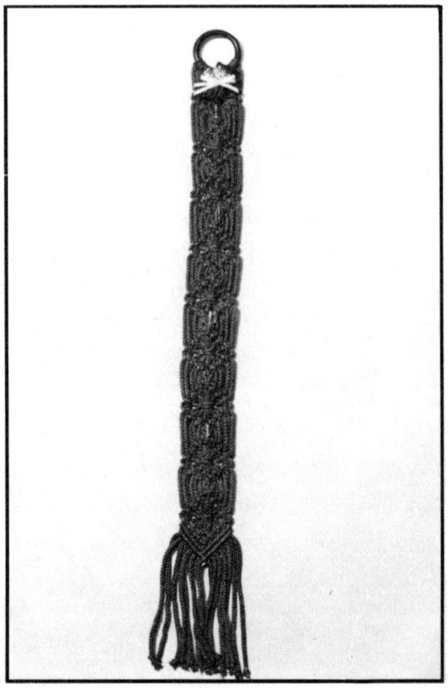

YOU WILL NEED:

one 3″ plastic ring
4 large, extra heavy pin-on drapery hooks
two 2″ pieces of cinnamon
10″ of 3/16″ wide feather edge ribbon in two colors
one 1″ pin backing
sprigs of dried filler flowers, like baby's breath
3 small silk flowers
craft glue
40 yards of 5-6mm cord

1

2

1 Cut the cord into eight pieces each 5 yards long. Fold each cord in half and attach to the plastic ring with a Reverse Lark's Head. Make nine diamond patterns, see page 2. Be sure to reverse the center 4 cords between each diamond.

2 Complete by following steps 8 thru 12 on page 4.

3

4

3 For the cinnamon bundle: glue the sticks together, then glue to the pin backing. Place the two ribbons together and tie a bow, glue to the cinnamon. Break off 1″ pieces of dried flowers, dip the ends in glue and tuck in above the bow. Glue the silk flowers as shown.

4 Pin the cinnamon bundle as shown. Insert one drapery hook between the first 2 diamonds. Drop down 2 diamond patterns and insert another drapery hook. Repeat with the last 2 hooks. Add the cups.

Door Chime

YOU WILL NEED:

one 3″ metal ring
3 bells of different sizes
20⅔ yards of 3mm braided cord

1

2

1 Cut the cord as follows: one cord 24″ long (save for step 20), four cords each 2¼ yards long and four cords each 2¾ yards long. Fold each cord in half and attach to the ring with a Reverse Lark's Head placing in this order—two 2¼ yard cords, four 2¾ yard cords, two 2¼ yard cords.

2 Do four rows of Alternating Square Knots, decreasing one Squre Knot in each row (see drawing on page 1).

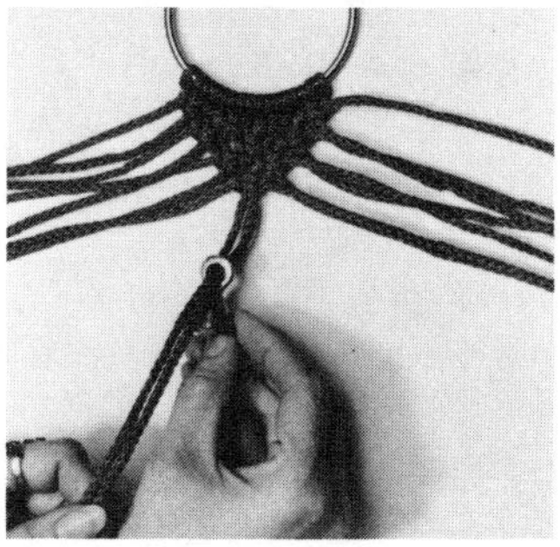

3

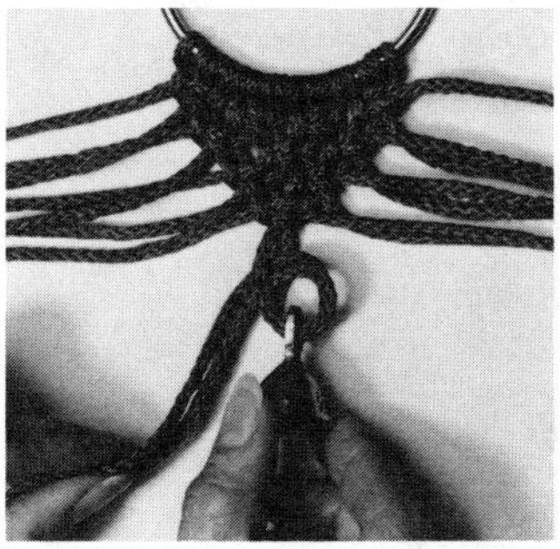

4

3 Attach the smallest bell by bringing the center two cords through the back of the bell.

4 Loop the cords as shown. Gently pull.

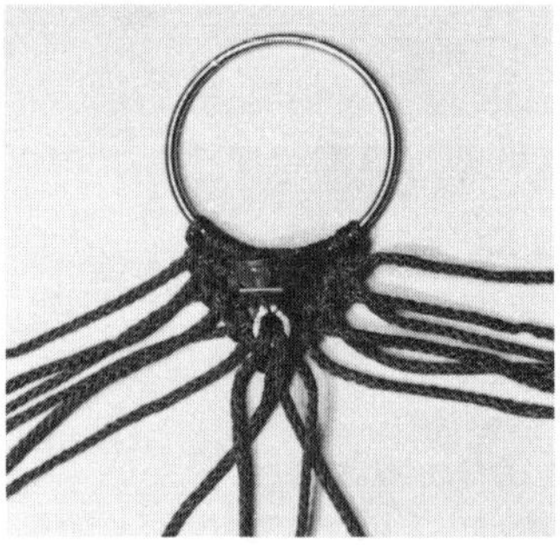

5

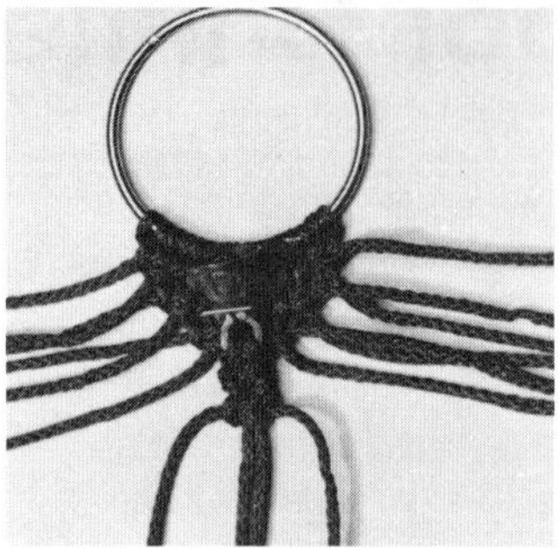

6

5 Pin the bell away from you. Lay cord 7 over 8 and cord 10 over cord 9.

6 Tie a Square Knot with the center 4 cords.

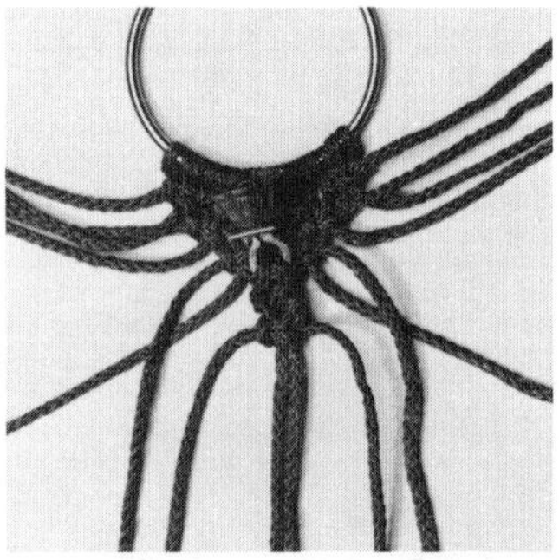

7

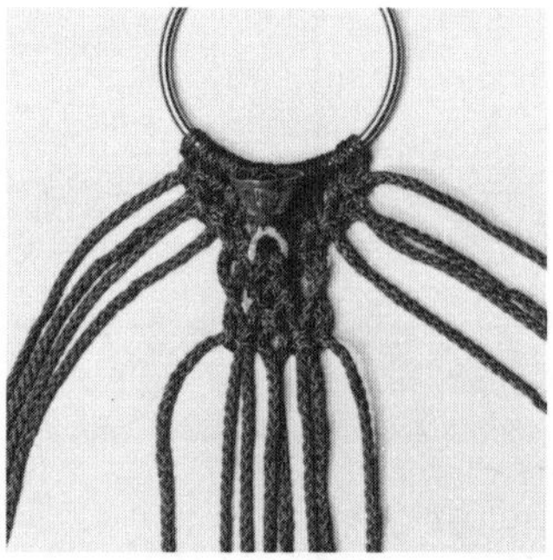

8

7 Lay cord 5 over the top of cord 6 and lay cord 12 over 11.

8 Tie two Square Knots as shown.

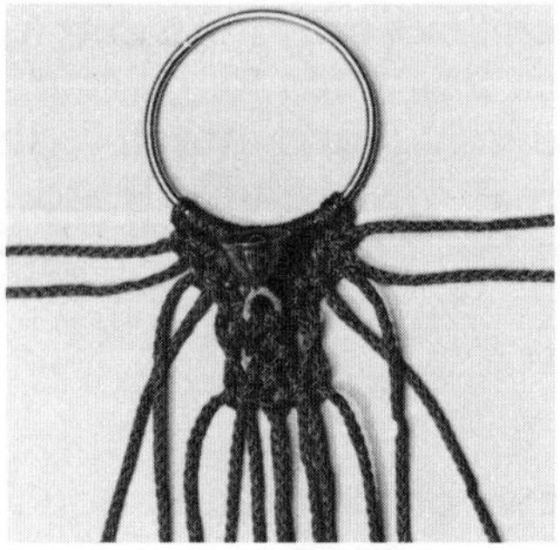

9

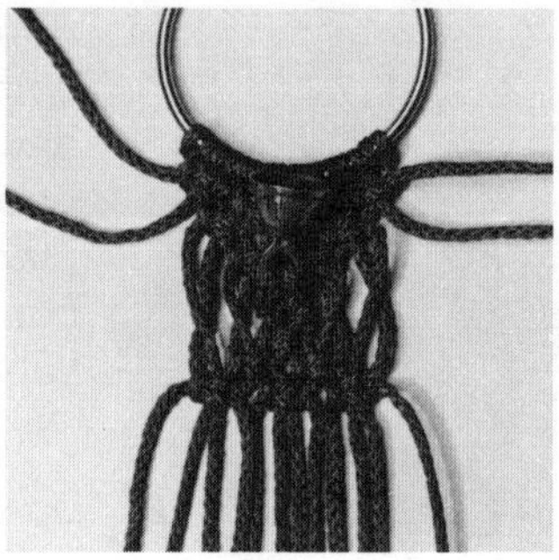

10

9 Lay cord 3 over cord 4 and lay 14 over 13.

10 Tie three Square Knots as pictured.

11

12

11 Lay cord 1 over 2 and lay cord 16 over 15.

12 Tie four Square Knots.

13

14

13 Tie three more rows of Alternating Square Knots, decreasing one Square Knot in each row.

14 Repeat steps 3 and 4 to attach the medium sized bell.

15

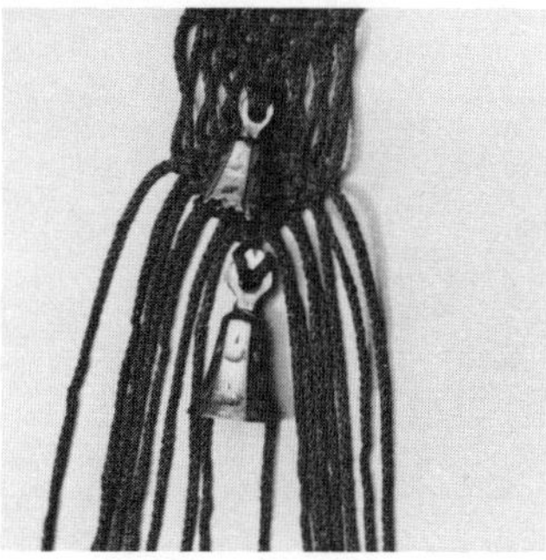

16

15 Repeat steps 5 thru 13.

16 Attach the largest bell following steps 3 and 4.

17

18

17 Repeat steps 5 thru 13 twice.

18 Finish the chime by following steps 8 thru 10 on page 4.

19

20

19 Gather all the bottom cords together. Notice the two end cords on either side are on top.

20 Wrap all cords with the 24″ piece of cord. Wrap eight times around the piece (see page 1). Pull each cord to straighten. Cut the cords to the desired length (6″ here). Comb or brush out the last inch of each cord.

Seasonal Swag

YOU WILL NEED:

one 1½" metal ring
three 2" jingle bells
pick (this one is plastic)
18 yards of 6–7mm or larger braided cord
2 yards of 1-3/8" wide (#9) ribbon
1 pipe cleaner

1

2

1 Cut off three cords, each 24" long and save for step 27. Cut four cords each 4 yards long. Fold in half and attach to the ring using a Reverse Lark's Head. Tie one Square Knot using cords 1, 2, 7 and 8 around the center four cords.

2 Tie two Square Knots using cords 1, 2, 3 and 4 then 5, 6, 7, and 8.

3

4

3 Lay cord 5 diagonally as shown. Double Half Hitch cords 4, 3, 2, and 1 over cord 5.

4 Lay cord 4 diagonally as shown. Double Half Hitch cords 6, 7 and 8 over cord 4.

5

6

5 Repeat steps 3 thru 6 two more times.

6 Tie a Square Knot with the center four cords.

7

8

7 With cords 1 thru 4 tie a Left Hand Square Knot, see page 1.

8 Tie a 2″ Left Hand Picot with cords 1 thru 4 as shown. Notice the cords extend 2″ to the left of the piece.

9

10

9 Tie a 2½″ Left Hand Picot.

10 Tie another 2″ Left Hand Picot.

11

12

11 Using cords 5 thru 8 repeat steps 9 thru 12 making Right Hand Picots.

12 Tie a Square Knot with the center four cords.

13

14

13 Lay cord 1 diagonally as shown. Double Half Hitch cords 2 thru 4 onto cord 1.

14 Lay cord 8 diagonally and Double Half Hitch cords 7, 6, 5, and 1 onto cord 8.

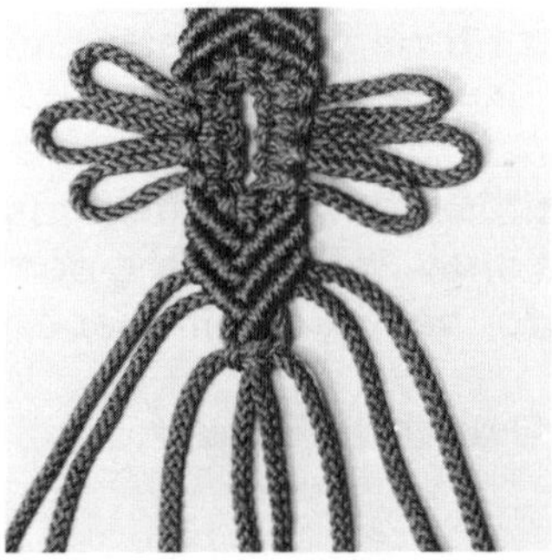

15

16

15 Repeat steps 15 thru 17 two more times. Tie a Square Knot with the center four cords.

16 Alternate and tie two Square Knots, using cords 1 thru 4 and 5 thru 8.

17

18

17 Tie another Square Knot using the center four cords.

18 Drop down 1″ and tie another Square Knot with the center four cords. Tie this knot LOOSELY.

19

20

19 Alternate and tie two Square Knots with cords 1 thru 4 and 5 thru 8.

20 LOOSELY tie another Square Knot with the center four cords.

21

22

21 Repeat steps 15 thru 17 twice.

22 Trim the middle two cords and melt the ends flush with the edge of the knots. (If available a soldering gun, wood burning or fusing tool work very well.)

23

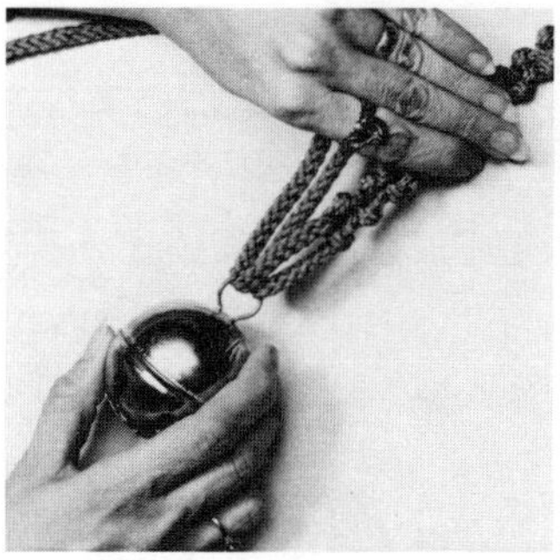

24

23 With the center two cords tie 8″ of Alternating Half Hitches. With the first 2 cords tie 4″ of Alternating Half Hitches. With the last two cords tie 6″ of Alternating Half Hitches.

24 String one bell onto the first Alternating Half Hitch Sinnet. Leave a 1½″ space and fold back the cords.

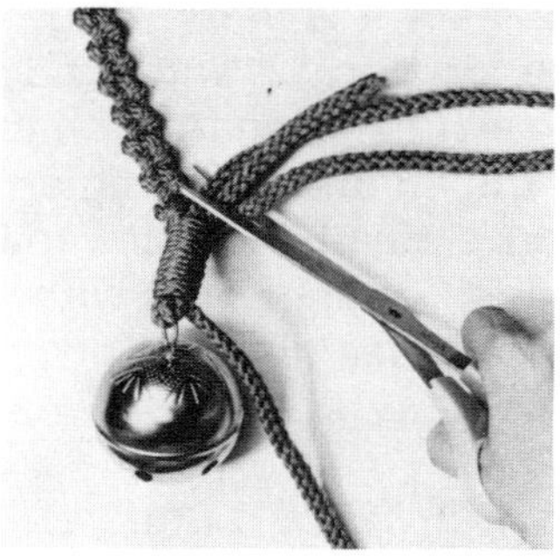

25

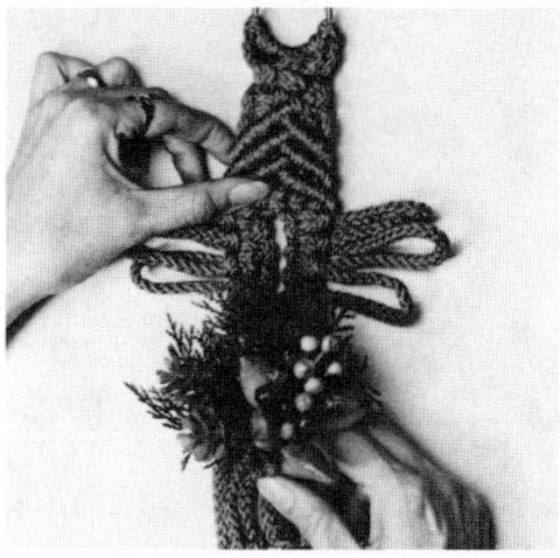

26

25 Use one of the 24″ cords from step 1. Wrap seven times (see page 1) and trim the excess length. Repeat with the other bells.

26 Insert the pick into the Square Knot as shown (remember these knots were tied LOOSELY). Trim the excess length of the pick.

27

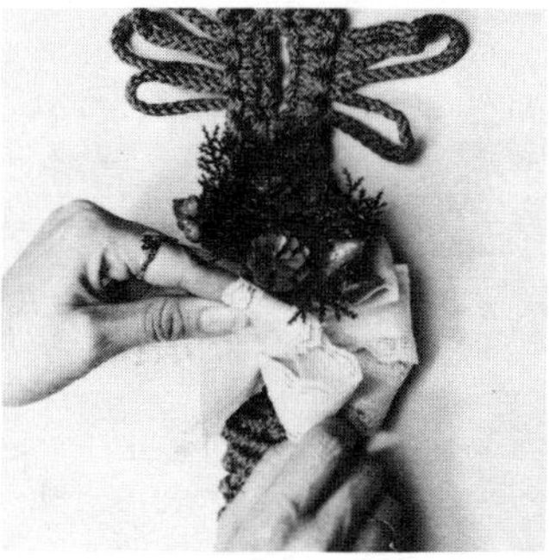

28

27 Make a bow, see inside the back cover. Slip a bow under the pick and tie in back of the macrame.

28 Spread open the ribbon.

Seagull Chime

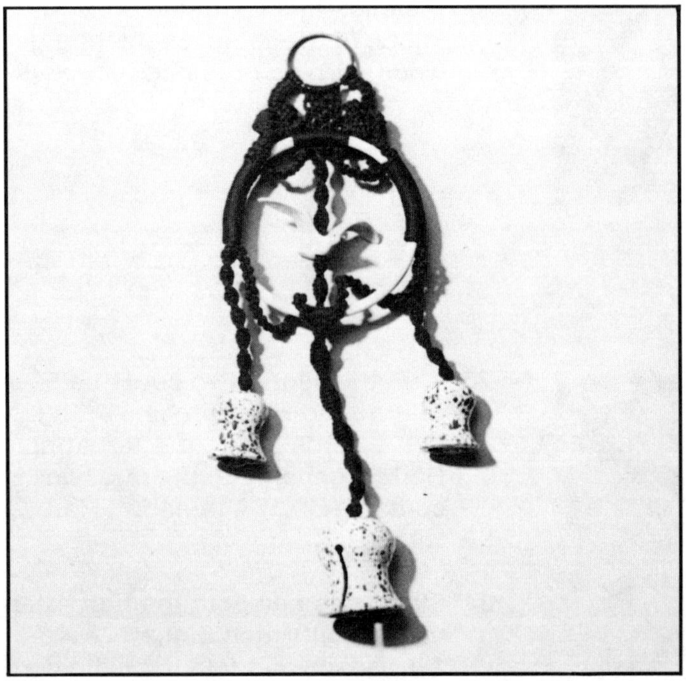

YOU WILL NEED:

one 2½" welded metal ring
one 7" plastic ring
1 large ceramic seagull (this one is 5" across)
two 2½" tall ceramic bells (the top hole should be no larger than ¼")
one 3½" tall ceramic bell (the top hole should be no larger than ¼")
34⅔ yards of 3 mm braided cord
three 12" pieces of #12 braided nylon fishing line

1

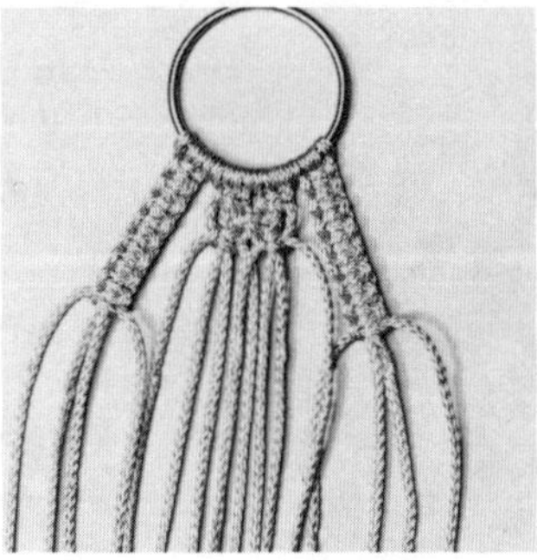

2

1 Cut 2 cords each 1⅓ yards long (save these for step 12) and cut 8 cords each 4 yards long. Attach the 8 cords to the metal ring using a Reverse Lark's Head. Tie three rows of Alternating Square Knots with cords 5 thru 12, see diagram on page 1.

2 With cords 1 thru 4 tie a Square Knot Sinnet of 8 knots. Repeat with cords 13 thru 16.

3

4

3 Pin left Sinnet as shown, and tie a Square Knot using cords 3 thru 6. Pin right Sinnet as shown and tie another Square Knot with cords 7 thru 10.

4 Tie three rows of Alternating Square Knots with cords 5 thru 12.

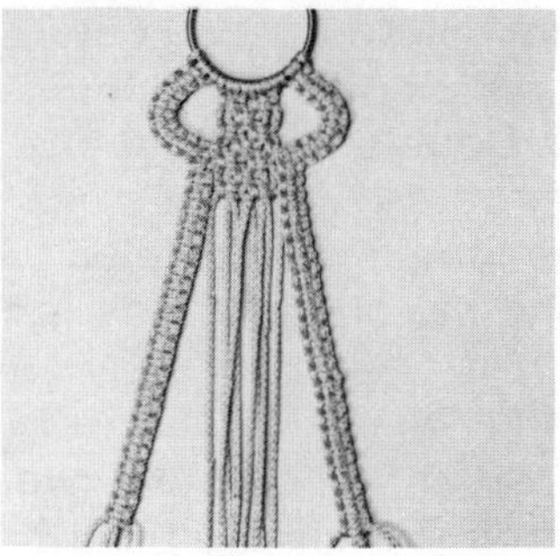

5

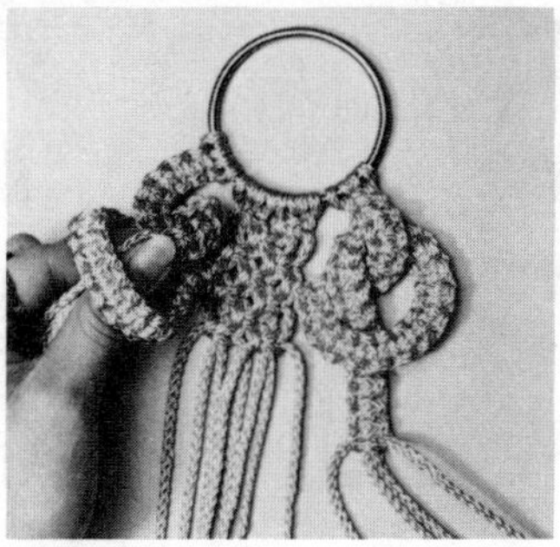

6

5 Tie a 7″ long Square Knot Sinnet with cords 1 thru 4 and 13 thru 16.

6 Using the 7″ Sinnet form a loop around the Square Knot Sinnet made in step 2. Repeat with the right Sinnet.

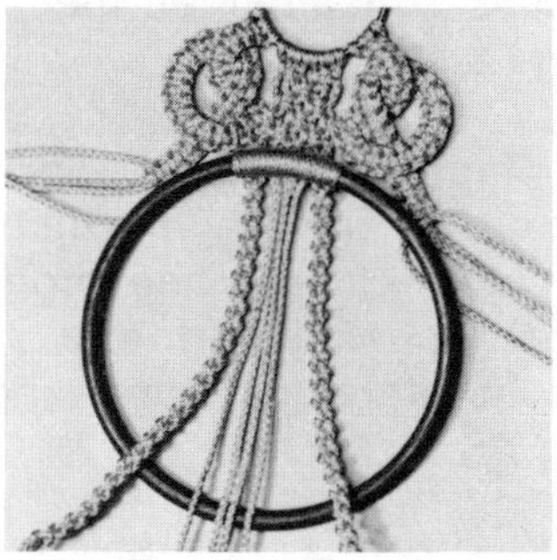

7

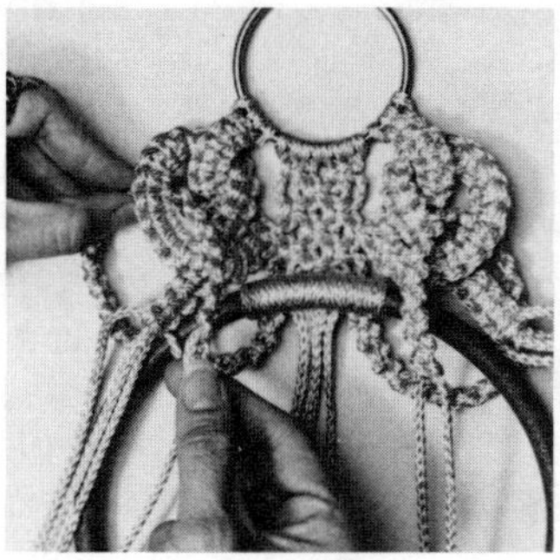

8

7 Double Half Hitch cords 5 thru 12 onto the 7″ plastic ring. With the first 2 cords on the ring make an 8″ long Alternating Half Hitch Sinnet. Repeat with the last 2 cords on the ring.

8 Bring the left Alternating Half Hitch Sinnet under the ring and through the Square Knot loop as shown. Repeat with the right Alternating Half Hitch Sinnet.

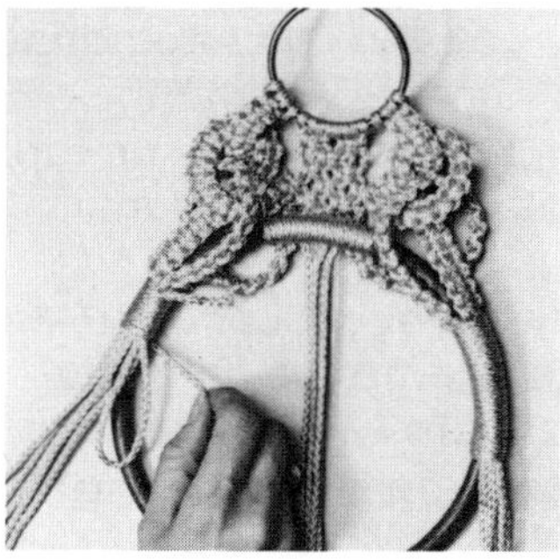

9

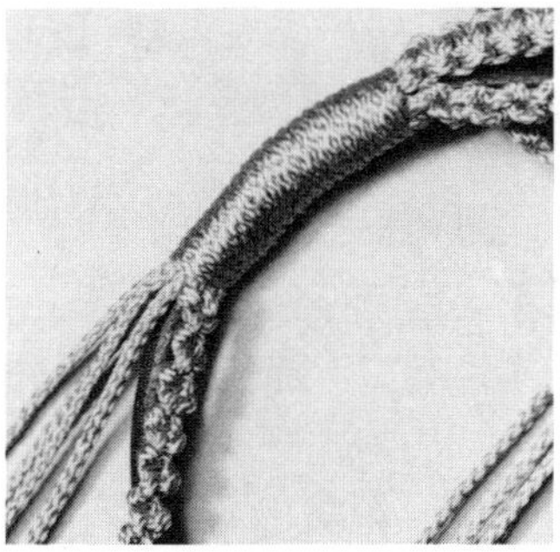

10

9 Position the left Sinnets as shown, notice the Square Knot Sinnet is on the outside. Wrap these Sinnets onto the plastic ring with a 1⅓ yards long cord cut in step 1. (The wrap should be 2½″ to 3″ long). Repeat on the right side.

10 On the left side, use the two longest cords and tie a 8″ long Half Knot Sinnet. Repeat on the right side.

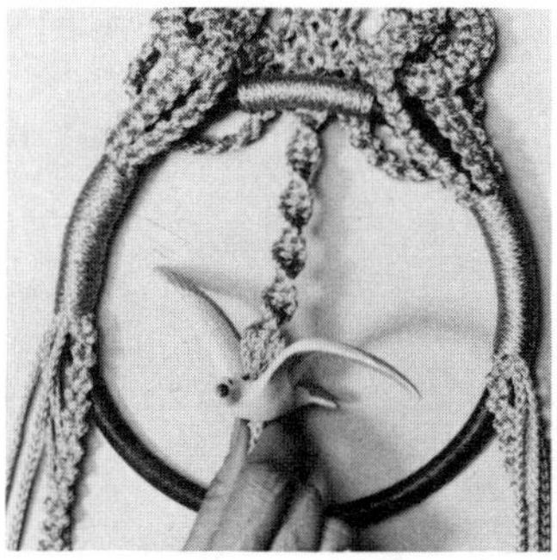

11

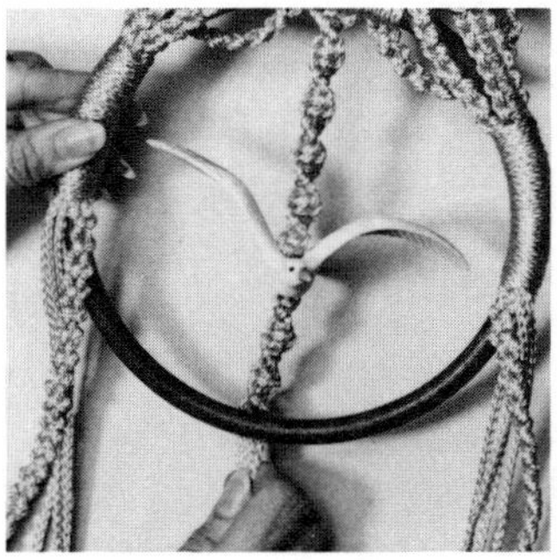

12

11 (It is easier to finish this piece when it is hanging from a hook, door knob or over a chair). With the 4 remaining cords in the center of the plastic ring, tie a 3½″ long Half Knot Sinnet. Slide the ceramic seagull onto the Sinnet.

12 Tie Half Knot Sinnets until it reaches the bottom of the plastic ring.

13

14

13 Double Half Hitch the two outer cords onto the bottom of the plastic ring. Then Double Half Hitch the two center cords on either side. Notice the longer cords are on the outside and the shorter cords in the center.

14 Slide the larger bell onto the two shorter cords. Tie an Overhand Knot so the bell will hang 8″ below the plastic ring. If necessary, make another Overhand Knot on top of the first one to prevent the bell from slipping. Trim and melt the ends of the cords.

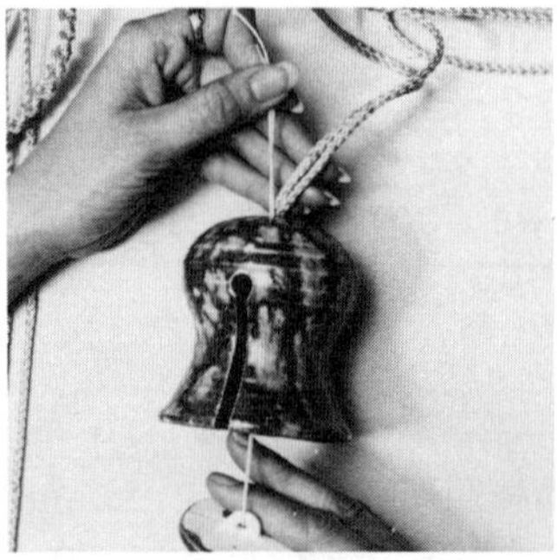
15

16

15 Slide the clapper onto a piece of fishing line. A crochet hook will be a help to pull the fishing line through the hole in the bell. Position the clapper so it hangs just inside the bell.

16 With the fishing line tie a Square Knot between the macrame cords as shown. Trim and melt the ends of the fishing line.

17

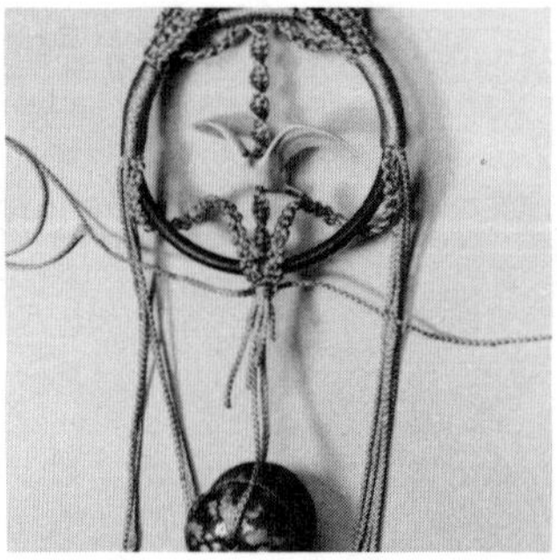
18

17 Loop the right and left Alternating Half Hitch Sinnets around the plastic ring as shown. Lay on top of the Double Half Hitch cords.

18 With the two longest cords, tie 3 Half Knots around the cords as shown. So there will not be a lump, trim the loose cords at varying lengths.

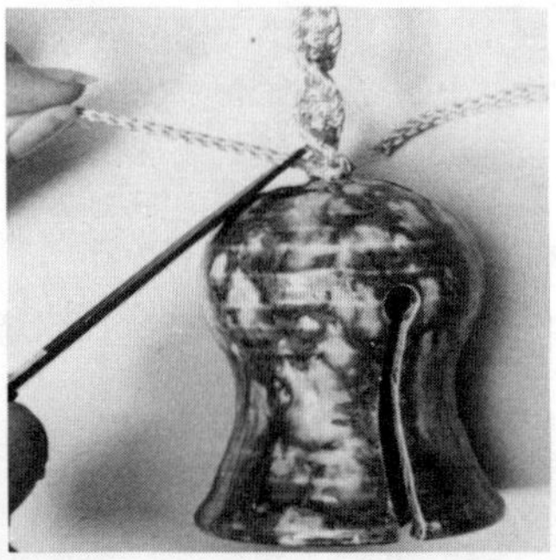
19

20

19 Continue tying Half Knot Sinnets until you reach the larger ceramic bell. Trim and melt the ends of the cords.

20 Repeat steps 14 thru 16 to attach the smaller bells so they each hang 6″ below the plastic ring. Finish by tying Half Knot Sinnets as in step 19, melt the cords.